How to Live Well

Simple and practical inspiration to enjoy your everyday life

FIONA FERRIS

Dedication

This book is dedicated to the lovely readers of my blog *How to be Chic*. Thank you for joining me in the pursuit of a simple and beautiful way of life.

Contents

Introduction

The concept of living well is one of my favourite subjects to think about. It encompasses every part of our life – how we live in our home, how we go about our days, what we wear and what we eat. Who do we spend our time with and who do we choose to share the intimate parts of our life?

We don't just need to float along though, taking what comes to us in life like we have no choice in the matter. We can intentionally design our life to be exactly what we've already dreamed of in our mind. Yes, it takes more effort than going along with the status quo and what your neighbours, friends and family might be doing, but there is real value in asking yourself 'what do *I* want'. I used to think this was selfish, but now realise it's not serving anyone if you go along with someone else's plan.

You don't need to upend your current life though. You can start small and look at the way you do things and the kinds of activities you participate in. Do they add to your life or detract from it? What would you rather be doing, you know, in that far away hazy perfect dream life in the future that always seems *just* around the corner? I've got news for you, that mirage will always be out of our reach if we don't call it forward.

Yes, it can feel scary, knowing we have so much power, but I know from the wonderful ways in which I've stepped into the unknown so far, you gain results that are incredible. And by being creative there are many ways you can elevate your lifestyle without spending much at all.

Chapter 1.

Looking forward to future plans

Even though I endeavour to make living in the present my main focus, we need to plan for the future too. So why not make it fun and exciting to think about?

In addition, rather than only looking forward to the big things – a vacation overseas or a new house or car perhaps – it is also inspiring to consider all the little things that we do every day, and make those as enjoyable as possible too.

Let's dive in.

On making the most of time

My husband and I own and run a retail footwear business. At this stage we don't have any staff, and we are open seven days a week. I update our website and do the bookwork, my husband does the ordering. We both see sales representatives with samples and both work in the shop.

All of this means we don't get a ton of time off together, as the shop would have to be closed. We are happy with it this way for now and, believe it or not we do still have balance in our life. We very rarely take work home with us and we have days off during the week which I actually prefer. They aren't with each other, but we do spend time together at work (we enjoy each other's company and have fun together as well as complete our work tasks).

A day off during the week mostly means a day at home for me (my absolute favourite place to be) or if I have some errands (rare, as decluttering cures the urge to shop, especially with our tiny house) it's so good to go shopping when most other people are at work.

If on the rare occasion I have to go to a mall, there are often lots of retired couples walking around, along with mums and pre-schoolers. I often think how nice it would be to be retired. Having an orderly, stress-free life. Spending all day doing the things you want to do, preparing for a meal, going out and gathering ingredients, browsing the library shelves, tending things at home.

I know I'm too young to think about retirement by at least twenty years, but when I'm out walking I go past a big new retirement complex nearby (which is more 'apartments to buy' than a rest home) and on the street-side is a big bay window looking into their communal living room. It is decorated with sofas that look like the Something's Gotta Give movie house, in fact the whole property is very chic and stylish and new but looks classic.

There are retired people in there who, no matter when I walk past are always talking and laughing and socialising. It's not far from our shop and I have often wondered what the minimum age is to move in. My husband is keen too! I sometimes wonder if we don't have more in common with these people than friends our own age.

We have no children, we like a tipple before dinner, we don't hold rowdy parties, a soft jazz CD is the loudest thing we play, we like our own space, we watch English soap Coronation Street and we rarely eat out. Plus I knit. Gosh, maybe I really am an 85 year old on the inside. On reflection, I think we actually already live like we're retired (except that we go to work, a minor consideration).

I also really like the couples they use in retirement advertising. They are walking along a beach, the wife has jeans rolled up with a white shirt. She is slender and chic with a silver bob. Her husband is handsome and lean with salt and pepper hair (perhaps more pepper) and has jeans on also with a V-neck navy jersey. Very classic and I can definitely relate to their style!

Paris is a goal. We did not have a honeymoon when we married just over two years ago, and our next (first) overseas holiday will be our Paris honeymoon. I don't care when that is, it could be ten years away. If this trip includes NYC so much the better. But I also think about retirement as a goal. It's roughly twenty-five years away for me and my husband as here in New Zealand sixty-five is the retirement age.

I don't want to fritter away time and money on mindless living. I did that in my twenties and thirties. Now that I am approaching my forties I have realised we don't have endless years on this earth. I plan to enjoy my time and plan wisely for the future.

All of this may sound really selfish, me, me, me, my enjoyment. But I have served others in the past, by volunteering at the SPCA for about four years before we had our own business. I had to quit because I couldn't be in two places at once. I donate money to favourite causes. It used to be Automatic Payments from my bank account, now I donate as and when I want to.

I also am in the process of using up my wool odds and ends and practicing my crochet by making rugs for needy babies. At my rate of crochet it could be a slow output but I'm doing something!

I also downloaded a knitting pattern from the SPCA for puppy sweaters. Apparently little abandoned puppies get extremely cold without their mother to warm them. So this is another plan for my wool scraps and tv time (I can't watch tv or a movie without knitting, crocheting, filing my nails etc. I get too fiddly and would likely go looking for something to eat).

So my goal for the next twenty-five years (and beyond) is to continue as I have started out:

Being healthy, strong and slender

Enjoying good, nutritious food cooked at home for the most part

Simplifying my life

Decluttering my home and paring down

Being a good steward of my money

Making the most of simple luxuries

Buying less but better quality, in food, clothing, furniture

Letting go of stressful notions that I can control the behaviour of others

Going with the flow

Nurturing my relationship with my husband – he comes before all other people in my life

Learn how to worry less, meditate. Anxiety is terribly aging

Learning not to worry about things I can't change

Appreciate all that I have – 'the less you want, the more you have'.

Embracing a new year

Even though it's only a date and another day, the New Year and actually, a new month or even a new week feels *different*. I'm excited at the year/month/week to come, and full of optimism of how I can better myself.

We have just been away on holiday. Our shop was closed for ten days and we were staying at a lovely, sleepy beach town a short drive from where we live. Our little poodle Atlas had a week in the country with my Poodle Rescue and retired poodle breeder friend Faye.

A beach town yes, but a beach town which has a twelve-level luxurious (to us) high-rise resort/apartment building, one block from a beautiful swimming beach and with Indian and Thai restaurants, a grotty yet fun bar and various shops within a two-minute walking distance. That's my kind of beach town.

As much as I've enjoyed our end of year holiday (I typed most of this in my bikini before going for a late morning swim) my head is full of possibilities back at home.

Coming home from being away somewhere (whether it's a decent length of time or a long weekend) I am always itching to get stuck into all the little projects I am planning (and have half-finished). I think it's imperative I go away on a regular basis just so I get things done!

My focus this year is *organisation*. By being more organised at home I can be more:

Serene

Relaxed

Slimmer

Calmer

Happier

I started decluttering within the last two years, and have gained a lot, but clutter creeps up on you doesn't it? My husband calls it recluttering when I come home from the Salvation Army charity store with a new candle, rustic basket or book.

And having my fortieth birthday in October and then Christmas - both times in which I've been given lovely gifts of course. Well, our small home is now bursting at the seams. I know, it's a very Western society problem to have when you have too many gorgeous things and can't move for them.

I am full of the possibilities of making our home very similar to the luxury high-rise apartment we stayed at the beach in. From the nature of holiday accommodation it isn't filled with the 'stuff' we have in our homes. It even has floor length white gauzy curtains which blow softly in the breeze, a la my ideal French girl Sabine's Paris apartment.

And of course I have Edith Piaf playing in the background while I dream of our sparsely furnished home where every cupboard and drawer is neat and organised.

This year I will have a 'Slim Pantry' like Anne Barone's. I have streamlined it fairly recently, but you can't do it once, it needs ongoing maintenance to straighten out and find unused items which can be incorporated into a meal.

I will also have a wardrobe tidy, in which I will divide into three sections:

1. Clothing which looks **fabulous** and is **comfortable** on me right now.

2. Clothing which I **love** but is maybe a little... **snug**... to be put away and tried on at a later date.

3. Clothing which looks **frumpy** and plain on me **at any weight** and/or is a **scratchy** fabric. This clothing is being boxed up and shipped out.

Over the coming months I will be visiting every cupboard, drawer and storage hidey-hole. I will be refining my possessions and using up what I've got, before going out to any store. I will be examining how I spend my time, and how I think.

Even though I could move right into a French-style decorated home, and have a number of gilt-type pieces around the house now, I am inspired most by simple, plain and airy homes like Tara Dennis shows. I have her book 'Home – Classic Essentials for Easy Living'. I will keep it to hand to remind me what I am aiming for.

I will not decide when I've made a small improvement that that is enough. As a procrastinator and a perfectionist I have to be bold and trust that I know best!

Dreaming up the ideal life

I am back at work now after a petite Christmas holiday. It's lovely and warm here in New Zealand and summer is definitely showing her sun-kissed face.

Since we went all out for our Hawaii trip last Christmas, we kept it a bit more budget-friendly and close to home this year. My darling and I embarked on a road trip that took us to Havelock North in Hawke's Bay where I grew up, then down to the city of Wellington for a few nights and finally we stopped in Martinborough, a bijou wine-growing district. Our entire trip was around 2,000km/1,250 miles and our final day we did almost 700km/435 miles! I haven't driven that far in a long time (well, been a passenger that far in a long time).

Despite the travel, our holiday was extremely relaxing and I read a few good books (including A Paris Apartment by Michelle Gable, which I did not want to end). I did get out of routine a little though. How can you not when you are away from home and doing different things and staying in different towns.

I enjoyed the walks I took but admit I did rather over-indulge in treat foods. Oh well, you have to do it every now and again to re-remember that yes, it might seem fun at the time but no, you still feel as unwell afterwards as you did the other times you did it...

Whilst I was out on one of my walks I got to thinking about life. What I thought about is that we spend most of our time working in a job, saving up money and paying off a house (if we're lucky), so we can sit back in retirement and enjoy our hard work. That's if we are still alive or in good enough physical shape to take advantage of our free time.

Yes, we all work hard (whether it's paid employment or not) and hope there is a payoff at the end of all that work, but that creates all the more reason to enjoy ourselves during our working life and not save up all the fun for 'one day'.

So I began to think of all the things I dream of doing one day when I'm retired and have all the time and money in the world (wouldn't that be nice) and use them for inspiration to live well *right now*. Here is my *Retirement Chic* inspiration:

The retirement me will be **fit, slim and healthy** because I have been committed to a lifestyle of nutritious food and regular exercise for a long time.

I might even have **a light tan** from daily potterings in our garden. Because the retirement me will be doing things such as weeding small areas at a time and tidying plants as I see them, we can enjoy park-like surrounds (that might be stretching it but it's nice to have a goal) on a daily basis. When I'm out walking it is so obvious the cared-for homes and gardens. It's not necessarily lots of money, but 'little and often' time spent on maintenance.

I also imagine our home being **clean, tidy and organised**. We will live in a place that is just the right size for us, and, I hope it is rural. In Martinborough we stayed in a tiny one-room cottage and it was so peaceful with no neighbours nearby, and a big open sky.

Naturally my retirement wardrobe will be a user-friendly and **stylish collection of clothing** in colours and shapes that flatter me, as I will have honed my style over the years. I think I am closing in on that style now actually, although I did the amateur's mistake of taking way too much with me on our trip. I did the same in Hawaii. That really is a skill I have to learn, but I go away so infrequently so can I use that as an excuse?

The ideal/dream/retirement me is **a writer**. How can I make that a reality? By writing daily and seeing how I can progress that.

So that's my vision of retirement, but really, what is stopping me from having and doing all these things right now? Of course I have the small thing called 'working in a shop five days a week' but surely I can work around this and make, as Tonya Leigh says '*the journey to the dream as beautiful as the dream itself.*

It just takes a little dreaming and planning.

Chapter 2.
Nurturing yourself

Whenever I feel tired out and like I have nothing left to give, it is because I have not been nurturing myself. Small things like going to bed at a decent hour, nourishing myself with good food and fresh water, and speaking as kindly to myself as I would a loved one go a long way to feeling fabulous.

Thankfully, just as quickly as you realise what you haven't been doing for yourself (because no-one else is going to do it if you don't), you can start those things again. Yes they might feel indulgent at first, but there's no glory in martyrdom.

Boudoir time

Anne Barone of the fabulous Chic & Slim book series mentions that chic French women take regular 'boudoir time'. This means withdrawing to their boudoir to take stock, recharge, and have quiet time alone.

My version of boudoir time is to go up to our bedroom after dinner but before bedtime. The bed is made and tidy, with pillows and cushions arranged in a pleasing way. All laundry is in the hamper, and clean clothes are hung up and put away.

I turn the bedside lamps on so there is a soft glow rather than the overhead light and spend thirty to sixty minutes or even longer reading. Often on my stomach or on my side laid out across the whole bed with either an old Victoria magazine (the French issues please) or some printed out internet inspiration (French Chic/Simplicity/Gentle Living etc) bound in a clear-file folder.

A glass of water or herbal tea is on the bedside table. Sometimes I will have a facial mask on, sometimes not, just a freshly washed face with night cream soaking in. I also massage a thick cream into neck and décolletage, hands and feet. A one-minute per foot self-massage is so dreamy and the cream helps keep your feet soft too.

As you can imagine, this time is a very relaxing prelude to drifting off to sleep. I really miss it when I don't make the time so I try to do it as often as possible. Even a mini-version is better than nothing.

It's sort of a transitional time between being awake and asleep.

Quiet time

I've been having quiet time lately.

Hardly any computer at home, lots of reading, sparkling water instead of wine, home-cooking and early nights. It feels wonderful and is just what I need. Quiet time counter-balances the manic-ness that is life in our shop. Trying to keep on top of everything is a nightmare at the moment.

But I do my best and know that when we step in the door at home, it's quiet time. I take the original idea of quiet time from school-children, where the teacher designates a time to slow down, be still and relax. Soft music may be playing to assist. Quiet pursuits like reading are encouraged.

Quiet time is good for the soul, and helps you rejuvenate to face the world again.

Blissful.

Low-stress secrets

I read a great article in the December 2010 Australian Women's Weekly. '*Real-life secrets of low-stress women* had the following tips, which I really found helpful. The bolded titles are from the article, and I have mostly paraphrased the information as well as adding my own thoughts.

Think friendly. Listen to your thoughts. Are they often negative? Do you speak to yourself in a way you wouldn't speak to a friend? I think negative thinking can be a habit we fall into, so when I catch myself I find it useful to think the positive opposite and I instantly start going in the right direction again.

Worry daily. Rather than spend all day (and night) worrying, write the worries down, and make a note of any action that could be taken. I find I do a less chic version of this. I stew and stew and let things get on top of me. Then I have a mini-breakdown and burden my husband with my woes. He makes sensible suggestions on how I can fit everything into my schedule (and never says unhelpful comments such as 'don't read blogs at work'), we make a plan and I'm happy again. Perhaps I could follow this advice, write my worries down and save him the stress.

Be grateful. Whatever you put your attention on expands and grows in your life. I've done the gratitude journal thing on and off for years since I first heard of it. I felt like a bit of a winner writing it down and thought imagine if someone read my lame writings, but I often say thank you to the Universe for lovely things or good luck. I also often think how lucky I am to have all that I do.

Eat chocolate. Dark chocolate is good for you. I know this because I can have it in the house without eating the entire block at once. That always means things are good for you. Popcorn, ice-cream, jubes and milk chocolate are not good for me. I can only eat 1-2 squares of dark chocolate a day, which I cannot say for popcorn, ice cream, jubes and milk chocolate. Therefore dark chocolate lives at my place while those others do not.

Take up yoga. I've already done this! I joined a class in the middle of last year. I started off going once a week and a few months in I upped it to twice a week. I had a break over Christmas of almost a month because the teacher was on holiday and I really missed it. I started back this week and I feel so good both during and after the class. I'm excited about an exercise that I enjoy and can see myself doing for the rest of my life. The magazine article said along with the facts that we know, like yoga increasing flexibility and toning muscles whilst calming the mind, is that yoga increases GABA, a brain substance which is often low in those who suffer from stress and anxiety.

Be honest. For most people lying is stressful, which is why lie detectors generally work. I heard a really cool quote recently that said 'sunshine is the best disinfectant' which I took to mean be honest, don't hide anything, and you'll feel better, healthier, happier. If you're worrying about what to say, just tell the truth.

Fall in love. The article stated that being married or in a long-term relationship alters hormones in a way that eases stress. I'm not sure that this belongs in my ideal list of low-stress secrets. Of course being in the right relationship is going to make you happier. But if you're with someone that isn't right, that can be worse than being single. And if you're single, you might feel you're missing out on a low-stress secret, when it's simply out of your control for now. You can work on yourself and be open and approachable, but it's not up to you when you meet your most excellent match. The Universe decides that. Let's kick this tip out of the list, it's too stressful. Let's go with things we can control.

Say hello to nature. This I agree with a lot. Years ago I replaced the gym with walking. I loved being outside amongst nature (even in town there are trees and gardens) more than I loved standing on carpet within walls, close to other people with loud bass music. Also, since adopting Atlas the elderly poodle, either my husband or I take five minutes every couple of hours to take a brief stroll along the grass verge. Little doses of vitamin D throughout the day! We also go for short-ish walks most days (about twenty minutes) to stretch his legs. Yesterday morning we had half an hour before we had to open the shop. Sometimes we go to a nearby cafe for a coffee (a real treat we do maybe once a week) but yesterday we walked through a nearby park. It was a lovely way to start the day.

Ask for help. Women have a tendency to try and shoulder the entire load and many of us are reluctant to ask for help. The article suggests we pick an area of our life where we could use the most help, ask the person or people we would like a helping hand from, and leave them to it. Mistakes will be made but that's part of handing over. Whenever I get the offer of help from my man and I'm tempted to say 'no that's ok I'll do it' I try and remember to say 'thank you' instead.

Eat foods rich in magnesium. I was told years ago that magnesium relaxes your muscles and helps you feel less tense. Naturally I went out and bought a magnesium supplement, which is fine, but you can also eat foods such as pumpkin seeds, brazil nuts, almonds and cashews as well as green vegetables. Another way to get it is take a bath with a handful of Epsom salts dissolved in it. Adding a few drops of lavender oil is recommended too. I'm not a fan of baths, but I do love nuts. I'll just have to remind myself to have them raw. Roasted and salted doesn't do their nutrition content any favours.

I would add to this list:

Be organised. Working on being more organised in my daily life and dealing with annoyances of my own making (such as leaving mending undone or ignoring a clutter hotspot) has made me feel infinitely happy, calm, serene and in control. Instead of walking past something twenty times before putting it away, I try and do it immediately. I'm also working on decluttering, creating good daily routines and home organisation. If I can find a place for everything and remember to put everything in its place, I will be one happy person.

Go to bed earlier. Only good things can come from this. I'm out of the habit of early nights at the moment and the times when I force myself to shut down the computer and wind down with a book before turning the light off nice and early I feel amazing the next day. My goal is for early nights to be the norm rather than the exception.

Breathe. Do you forget to breathe? I do. I find myself not exactly holding my breath, but I'm holding onto something. To lower stress, let your breath flow in... and out. And when you breathe, your stomach should expand not your chest. I think as females we are so used to holding our stomach in that we train ourselves to breathe in a counter-productive way.

Live within your means. 'Annual income twenty pounds, annual expenditure nineteen six, result happiness. Annual income twenty pounds, annual expenditure twenty pound ought and six, result misery'. - Charles Dickens. I know first-hand how horrible it feels to spend more than you have and then dread the credit card statement. It is such a good feeling to know you have money in the bank to cover your bills, plus an emergency fund of X months of living expenses (start with one month and work your way up to six to nine months seems to be the advice given by financial professionals).

How to feel better

After our dear rescue-poodle Atlas died (aged fifteen, excellent effort little fellow), I felt quite down, and this carried on to a general flatness and loss of interest in things that usually excite me. I also felt a little burnt out and detached from others.

I've never had proper depression but from time to time, right back to my teens I have had the occasional bout of mild melancholia. It's also mid-winter here so that may have something to do with it, even though I normally love the cosiness of winter.

I know it will pass with time, but meanwhile I've been doing the following to help it on its way.

Being gentle with myself, not doing too much if I don't want to. Rather than a whirlwind marathon housework day (which I just don't have the energy for at the moment) I do the basics and spend some time pottering, sewing, reading and relaxing.

Having early nights. I start winding down about 9pm and am in bed reading well before 10pm lights out. I've been sleeping like a log thank goodness. I also find I feel worse in the evening, so it's nice to wash my face good and early and hop into bed. I think my body needs lots of good, pure rest. One night last week I made noises about heading off to bed. 'But it's only ten past eight!' my husband said incredulously. That was quite funny. I managed to last until nine.

Not medicating with food and drink. When I did decide to let loose with food and drink, I felt a lot worse. Being in control of my diet and my weight goes a long way towards feeling happier.

Remembering to breathe. Often I find myself holding onto my breath. It feels such a relief to let it flow in, and out. I need to remind myself many times a day.

Keeping to my daily routines.

Talking to someone. I told my husband last night I was feeling low. I feel better for having shared it, he had some helpful suggestions, and now he is looking out for me too.

Yoga twice a week. I have missed it a few times lately and have been only attending once a week. I'm sure this has not helped my low mood as I always feel great - energised, relaxed and positive after a yoga workout.

Walking outside. I walk to yoga and back, and I also like to do errand walks on foot as long as it's not pouring with rain. A light sprinkle is ok, I take an umbrella. I met two old colleagues for lunch one day last week, and walked to meet them. It was the next suburb over and took about 45-50 minutes each way but it meant I didn't have to find a park, and got some exercise and fresh air at the same time. It was inner-city too so quite interesting.

Reading. I have been alternating my positive thinking books with pure escapism (currently the first Sophie Kinsella Shopaholic book – that series had me laughing out loud they are so crazy).

Also **escapism tv/movies**. Nothing gritty or real for me I'm afraid (now or at any other time). Keeping up with the Kardashians and the Real Housewives of Beverly Hills are great medicine I find. Not hours on end though. Just an episode here and there. I also like to re-watch favourite feel-good fun movies at times like this.

Clearing out clutter corners at home and at work. If an area is bothering me, even if I have other things to do, I attack the clutter corner. It often only takes a small amount of time, and I feel infinitely better and more able to tackle the harder jobs instantly. I went through all my trays at work on Saturday, filing and throwing out. A clear in-tray is a thing of beauty isn't it? Even if it doesn't last very long, but I *will* keep on top of it.

Taking vitamin C. I go through phases of taking vitamins, and at the moment I don't take any, but I always have vitamin C in the cupboard for when a cold threatens to come on. I read in a model beauty book ages ago that models take a 2000mg dose of vitamin C to give them a boost. As shallow as I am, I have been taking the models advice.

Be 'selfish' and **say no**. No to library books that don't hold my attention, no to tv programmes or movies I have taped and decided I don't like. It feels hard to do, and I don't like to let people down, but learning to say no is so beneficial to our mental health. If I get a niggling feeling in my stomach when I think about something, I have been making a decision there and then to do something about it properly (not just putting it off).

Indulging in the little luxuries. I use all my lovely things and don't feel guilty at all.

Don't go shopping! No good purchasing decisions could possibly be made so I've been staying away from the shops.

Daydream about the future. I do this both by myself by writing down lists of my ideal lifestyle, home, personal style, person I want to be, and with my husband about what type of home we want to purchase, what we would do with tons of money if we won the lottery (not that we take out tickets, but still, it's fun).

Plan ahead little treats. We are booked into our favourite five-star luxury hotel right here in the city we live in a month or so's time. Just for a night. They always have good package deals and it's a mini-break we can still have while running a seven-days-a-week business. Looking forward to going really is half the fun.

Actually, I'm starting to feel a little bit better already. Have I missed anything off the list? What makes you feel better when you're low? I wonder what a chic French woman would do to combat malaise?

Recipe for a good night's sleep

We have finally employed someone apart from my husband and myself in the shop. She is wonderful and with us three days a week, but it still seems like I am always catching my tail.

Yesterday I had a day off at home to bless our abode with cleanliness and order. Looking forward to a day such as this, where I go nowhere and see no one (except for our rescue-cat Miss Jessica, who is my little shadow), makes me realise how much I love living a routine and simple life.

When life gets hectic, I realise I invariably end up going to bed too late. Often it is not from doing a job which needs to be done, but just because I am fluffing around. Perhaps if I feel rushed and busy, going to bed early makes me feel guilty because there is something else I could be doing?

I like to make a conscious effort to take these steps in order to have a good rest and wake refreshed the next day.

- Early dinner (served around seven is early for us), one glass of wine maximum, or sparkling mineral water

- Computer turned off before dinner/no computer after dinner or at least 1 hour before bedtime (not only does the lit screen wake up my brain, but I find myself click-click-clicking my time away)

- Take plenty of time for my bathroom routine – makeup removal, cleansing and moisturising, brush and floss teeth.

- Read after dinner instead of the computer or tv, with a cup of tea and lights out well before ten pm.

Chapter 3.
Living a life of style

Call me shallow, but I do love thinking about the concept of living a life of luxurious style. I don't necessarily want to spend a lot of money, and I'm always looking around for inspiration on how to elevate my life (while still keeping the simplicity that I crave) to one of high style on a minimal budget.

Living a chic life

With my interest in all things chic, how could I pass up a book entitled 'Chic - life as it should be'. Stylish and authoritative. One reviewer said the author Colin Cowie made Martha Stewart look like a slob, and reading this book confirms that as a fact. Apart from writing books, he is a very highbrow events co-ordinator.

It is a very inspiring read, and makes me get up and declutter a shelf after finishing a chapter. For example, rather than have a bedside table cluttered with everything you could ever want to reach for, Colin has the top drawer all but empty, with the essentials laid out on one of those lacy thin rubber mats cut to fit the drawer (to stop everything sliding around).

For me, body butter, hand cream, lip cream, lip balm, pen and paper, mini alarm clock and a few other bits and pieces (like my bookmark collection so I always have a pretty one to use). And then you would have a few choice items on the top. He said his goal is to have his home look like a chic hotel.

This book also has many pictures of Colin's home in NYC. His style is a little masculine for me, however I can appreciate the stylish orderliness and I covet his labelled, stacked, grouped closets and cupboards.

Here is a wonderfully motivating excerpt from the book:

The foundation of any well-run home is cleanliness and order. An orderly house will not only give you pleasure, it will also make everything in your life, from writing a thank-you note the day after a fabulous evening to opening your home to over-night guests, that much more effortless.

Living elegantly means creating a place you look forward to coming home to, a place where you can entertain happily, harmoniously, and generously.

If my home is in order, I feel as though my life is in order and I can take on anything. I love walking into an intelligently designed, immaculate kitchen. I love opening the freezer door and finding everything I need neatly stacked: frozen appetisers ready to be popped into the oven, decorator ice cubes available to enliven a chic cocktail, chicken stock waiting to form the base of a delicious home-made soup.

In the closet, I love finding my shirts arranged from light to dark, short-sleeve to long, beautifully starched, and hanging from matching hangers. I love clean, polished surfaces that are stripped of any unnecessary clutter. I love opening my desk drawers and immediately finding business cards, personal stationery, pens, and my cell phone charger. And at night, I love retiring to a bedroom so pulled together and luxuriously welcoming that I could easily mistake it for a five star hotel suite.

Keep the things that are precious to you close by and available so they can be used on a regular basis. Everything else should be stored in a safe place, not left out on display. Serving bowls should be on the tables only when they're overflowing with food, and there's nothing at all exciting about an empty vase perched on a windowsill (even if it's Lalique!). Less is definitely more!

For example, a simple vase with one exotic flower on a central table can be more astonishing than that same vignette surrounded by fourteen framed pictures and half a dozen objets *from your last European vacation.*

Instead, keep a separate closet or cupboard where you can store your collection of decorative items. When you bring them out for entertaining, they'll seem brand new again. Use your pieces to create varied and interesting vignettes and fresh atmospheres, then put them away for the next time the mood strikes.

Invest in drawer dividers, baskets, and closet organisers. Trays and decorative bowls can also be fantastic containers for odds and ends such as keys and loose change. Create areas for everything you use, which will allow you to find what you're looking for when you're looking for it.

Try to take twenty minutes each day to tidy up and put things back where they belong. When you're having a few friends over for drinks or throwing a party, you shouldn't have to do a major all-day cleaning. The longer you delay straightening up, the more burdensome it is to clean. It's much better, and a lot less overwhelming, to maintain order and cleanliness as you move through your day.

Granted, most people work and have to scramble to keep up with household chores. But ideally, you'll get to a point where with a bit of soap and water, a mop and a broom, some dimmer switches on the lights and a little music, your home should be ready to receive guests at practically a moment's notice. A little at a time goes a long way.

--

I saw Colin and his partner on Oprah and he was so engaging and funny I couldn't help but liking him. His partner said if he ever wants to upset Colin all he has to do is shake a drawer so everything gets mixed up. Colin may sound a little OCD-ish but he makes it seem so appealing.

I think Colin's advice to take a small amount of time to tidy up each day is so wise. It really makes a huge difference to both the smooth running of my household, and my levels of serenity. I also changed my bedside table to reflect Colin's recommendations two and a half years ago when I first read the book, and it is still like that today. It must be working.

Elegance is refusal

When I first heard the Coco Chanel quote *elegance is refusal*, the first thought that came to me was food. That I had to refuse food to become elegant and trim like the bird-like Mademoiselle Chanel. And being a food-lover there was no way I could picture myself eating tiny portions so I've always had a bit of a block towards these words.

Lately and from two different sources I have heard of a more enticing way to look at it, which ties in perfectly with my love of curating a beautiful life by decluttering items that do not fit the vision of the lifestyle I have for myself.

And that is just it – refusal of anything that does not elevate your life to exquisite elegance.

Refusing junky foods in favour of high quality fresh foods.

Refusing possessions that detract from rather than add to my enjoyment of life. And this includes refusal of excess possessions. We all like different ways of living, but I feel at my most content when I have less around me.

Refusing clothing that does not make me look and feel chic and sophisticated. That includes clothing I wear to work or out, loungewear at home, nightwear and lingerie. Everything!

Refusing to be around people that bring me down or make me feel bad about myself.

Refusing to accept others beliefs as gospel. I'm cultivating my own wonderful and empowering beliefs thank you very much.

Refusing negative thoughts because they don't feel good *and* they weaken your immune system. Apparently it's been proven in tests which gave me a jolt when I heard that.

Refusing to listen to myself when I say something is too big or scary to entertain. What could I achieve if I believed I could do that huge achievement. Why would I block it from my mind immediately? Even if I never do it, I've at least not closed my mind to it.

Chapter 4.
Chic habits

It is the little things that you do on a daily basis that are so important, because these are the moments that make up your life. There is no one big thing we are waiting for, believe it or not, and it's the habitual way we live our lives that gives it its flavour.

Switch unhelpful habits out for habits that improve your life and watch how you suddenly start heading in the direction you desire. It's as simple as that!

Go to bed earlier, get up earlier

For the past several years, I have been getting up an hour earlier, all so I can drink hot tea with milk and read – usually blogs, less often a book or magazine. I can have a lovely time catching up on all my favourite blogs and do my own writing. It's now routine for me to get up earlier and I absolutely love this time.

In the height of summer when I started doing this it was lovely and light already, but as we creep towards Autumn it's a little dark at first (I get up around 6-6.30am, not that early compared to a lot of folk. Our shop doesn't open until 9.30am so we often leave for work around 9am) but I still enjoy this early time, even if the blinds are still down and the lights are on for the first part.

It's guilt free time too. I know it's not good to surf the net when at work – there are important things to do there, and being self-employed I'm not doing myself any favours. And in the evenings I feel like a terrible wife glued to the laptop screen while my husband is sitting by himself on the sofa. So I get my fix first thing. And I've restarted my 'book', you know, the book we're all writing. I feel like a bit of a fraud writing, I don't know why. But I love reading so much and I have told myself – even if no one else reads it. Write a book you would like to read.

One I just finished and which I enjoyed immensely is A Spring Affair by Milly Johnson. I do love chick lit to relax and escape – there is so much uninspiring formulaic stuff out there though that it's exciting to find a new author. Some I love are Sophie Kinsella (all of them), Emily Giffin (all of them) and Emily

Barr (have only read Plan B but loved it – and it had a French angle).

I picked up A Spring Affair from the library new releases shelf and upon reading the back cover found it was, ta da, a new genre 'decluttering chick lit'. Imagine! I had to borrow it of course and found it was such a lovely, funny, enjoyable book which actually had me in tears over my breakfast at the end. I love those books! And it had decluttering advice all the way through. A book tailor made for me I think. And maybe you too if you're a chick lit fan and as obsessed with decluttering as I am.

I went to the author's website after I had finished and apart from a section on decluttering (yay), found tips for budding authors. If nothing else, she said, write 250 words per day, no matter what, and at the end of the year you will have a 91,000 word book. And don't edit, just keep writing. Edit right at the end otherwise you will lose momentum. So that's what I'm doing in the morning now. Before I start anything else, I write at least 250 words and then I am free to read all those inspiring blog posts.

So I can heartily recommend going to bed earlier and getting up earlier. After all, what do you do in the last hour of the evening anyway, lie there on the sofa thinking I'm too tired to get up and wash my face, watching tv that isn't even any good, nothing actually productive. Sometimes I do that exact thing and go to bed at 11pm. That's only 7 hours sleep – not nearly enough! I like to start getting ready for bed around nine and be in bed reading by 9.30-10. I aim for nine hours sleep like apparently French women get, but eight is a good minimum.

How to stay young

I wish there was a tape recorder going for the conversation I had with this customer, because I don't think anyone will believe me when I relay it to them.

A nice, well-dressed lady was buying a pair of shoes, and said she needed them to get around in the weekend and watch the grandchildren play rugby on a Saturday morning.

'Grandkids!' I spluttered. 'You look too youthful to have grandkids, what's your secret?' I asked her. After I said it I realised it may be misconstrued as an impolite question (starting very young etc). Luckily she didn't take offence.

'What cream do you use?' I quizzed. 'None really', she said 'I don't use much at all.' 'Good genes?' I asked again. 'No, that's not it. My mother has a lot of age spots'.

After a bit she said 'Sex! Lots of sex. I'm not joking. Have sex. And have it a lot.'

Cue my startled face and then an interesting conversation. I'm no prude but she was very upfront and happy to tell me her secret to defying her age. And ten minutes before I'd never met her.

I told her about an Oprah show I saw a while back about a couple who were overweight, tired out and unhappy. They decided to rev up their life by making a pact to have sex every day for a year. You can imagine how vibrant, trim and healthy this couple looked after the year was up, not to mention happy and smiling, with an enviable energy.

'It would be hard if you were single though' I put to her. 'Oh, my friends think I'm terrible' she said, 'but I have a 'friend' who's ten years younger than me and we've been getting together for a couple of years. I've had marriage and I've had long term relationships, I just can't be bothered with those now. I'm happy being single and just getting together with my friend every so often.'

I admit I was a little speechless (and impressed with her candour) at this stage. She recommended sex as the best exercise you can have, and of course it is fun and free.

Just in case you are wondering otherwise, she wasn't tacky or tarty looking. She just looked like a pleasant, normal woman who might be standing in front of you at the supermarket checkout. Except that you might think she was 45 when she was really 55. I didn't have the cheek to ask her age, but I was dying to know.

She asked if I always worked Fridays and I said I did, as she wanted to come in again for another pair of shoes and would come when I was there. Maybe I'll find out then.

Swapping stockpiling for tranquility

I know this is such a 'first world problem' to have, but in our Western culture of stocking up, stockpiling and overstocking, there is something very satisfying of *having just enough*.

I used to love stockpiling bargains on consumables such as pantry food items and toiletries. But now in an effort to live more simply and have less noise around me, I've tempered my ways.

I'm embarrassed to say there have been times when I've gone overboard and it has taken us months to plough through whatever specially-priced item I stocked up on.

Our big box supermarkets often have enticements to 'spend $200 and receive a petrol discount voucher' which has regularly encouraged us to see what we need and stock up on it. But in a household of two people and two cats, we really have to try hard to spend $200 in one go. It was quite stressful just to gain a coupon that saved us about $10-12 (which isn't to be scoffed at, I agree, but not worth it if you are crowded out of your house with grocery items that might not be used for many months, if at all!)

So I gave myself permission not to stockpile. I gave myself permission to let something run out and see if I missed it. Sometimes I did and sometimes I didn't. It is quite a lovely feeling to see space in the pantry and see what items I can use up to make a delicious dinner.

It is also refreshing to know that I can use up my many skincare and cosmetic items before I even need to think of perusing another specials brochure. *I don't even need to look at that brochure because I already have enough skin cream/shampoo/body lotion.*

Speaking of body lotion, a couple of months ago I bought a 5 litre (1 1/3 gallons!) container of body lotion from a local skincare factory shop, how funny is that. But I do go through it is vast quantities.

It's quite fun to see how many days we can *not* go to the supermarket, and if we need something, it's put on the shopping list for when we really, really need to go.

We often pop into fruit and vegetable stores to get fresh produce, but the supermarket list can wait for quite a number of days until we have to go. And it still might only be less than a dozen items. It's such a thrill not to have armfuls of grocery bags to bring into the house. Plus, there is not money coming out of my wallet while I'm doing this.

When you think about it, I must live a pretty sheltered life if *not stockpiling* is acting in a risky way, so I feel very lucky about that. Many people in other parts of the world would *wish* this was their most pressing concern.

Are you a stockpiler? Bargain hunter extraordinaire? Does the thought of having space on your bathroom/kitchen/ laundry shelves make you nervous? 'Not-stockpiling'. It's the new way to save time, sanity and money don't you know.

Cultivating calmness

'Make inner peace your highest goal and you will probably never make another mistake.' – Brian Tracy

I heard this listening to an audiobook by my friend Brian Tracy when I was driving home from work a few days ago. I wrote it down at the next red light and put it in my little French Chic notebook when I got home. I have been repeating it to myself since I first heard it and it has been so helpful and comforting.

Getting worked up over little things always makes me feel awful and I know it's not good for me, both mentally and physically. Now that I have taken on board to 'make inner peace my highest goal', situations that I would have become quite annoyed with were simply smoothed over and I felt much better about everything afterwards even though 'by rights' I should have been bothered about something.

In an instance where I feel myself becoming peeved over a minor annoyance, I repeat the saying to myself and instantly feel transformed. Inner peace is a wonderful thing to strive for and I'm going to use Brian's saying almost as my life motto.

I was at the supermarket just before, and I noticed I was overcharged for two items. I went to the customer services desk and was told I was wrong. I was sure I was right but after querying them a bit more and them telling me I could ring the toll-free number for their head office to check it out, I said I trusted them, and left the store.

I had planned to call the head office once I got to the car 'for my own peace of mind' to know if I was incorrect or they were. By the time I opened my car door I had been repeating my new mantra to myself and realised it wasn't worth the $1.89 difference to me (even though I believe the saying that if you look after the pennies the pounds will look after themselves).

I could see me spending time on hold and getting myself all churned up talking to someone trying to prove I was right. It wasn't worth it! Making inner peace my highest goal saved the day and I was calm as I drove home.

I read about Kim Cattrell in an English magazine (Woman & Home, May 2013). She was being interviewed, among other things, about how incredible she looks for her age. This is what she said:

When I hit my forties I thought, 'I can't play a sexy siren anymore.' Almost 20 years later, it's still going on. I think that's because I take care of myself, which includes dieting, exercising and minimizing stress.

I joke that I've been on a diet since 1974, which is basically true. I like to eat, and my body type is not naturally this thin, especially at this age. So I do watch what I eat and drink but I'm not obsessive –

it's just a way of life. So I don't have dessert after every meal – I just can't do it.

I have a big appetite, and staying on top of that is about knowing myself and saying, 'I can eat that today but tomorrow I'm not going to.' And I'm always aware – from gaining and losing weight for parts – that the time in the gym trying to lose extra weight is really hard work! I always have that in my mind.

Apart from the fact that I was impressed with her honesty, I thought it was so interesting that she included reducing stress in her life as one of her keys to staying slim, healthy and youthful-looking.

You often hear celebrities talk about meditation and I even bought myself Meditation for Dummies which actually is a wonderful book. But I still would get all righteous and worked up over small injustices in daily life and the meditation book couldn't fix that.

I always felt like I wanted everything to be fair. It was easy when I was the one who had to tell the truth, give back the wallet I found with $400 in it, own up to a mistake and all those sorts of things. But when it's the other person who should be 'giving in', well, you can't control that and it's stressful when you try!

So as good as my meditation book was, it didn't help me be calm in various situations. My 'new life motto' does. It helps me see the truth and live a peaceful life.

It applies to any and every situation that I have tested it on so far and I am very thankful that I came across it.

Chapter 5.
Inspiration on living well

If you've ever lacked *motivation* to do something that you desperately want to achieve and can't quite get there, why not try it from the other way – use *inspiration* to help you get what you want. It's pulling you towards something rather than you trying to push yourself, and is far more effective. Save your energy for where it is needed elsewhere!

Following are my favourite petite essays inspired by the thought of living well. We each have our own idealistic lifestyle – these show you mine. I hope they will be helpful in your journey of refining how you want your life to look and feel.

Living a small life

The more time I spend on this earth, the more I realise I can please myself and be myself. I don't need to pretend to want great things and I don't need to fret that I've never had or probably never will have a high-powered career.

I've come to realise that's not what I'm about. I enjoy a quiet and simple life. Ever since I left school I've always worked at 'normal' office jobs. I didn't attend University because I didn't really know what I wanted to study, and I didn't want to go just for the sake of it. So I started my first full-time job at eighteen (although I had already been working part-time after school and in school holidays since I was fourteen) and have been working ever since.

My husband and I now own a small retail business which we started almost seven years ago. We have decided for now we are content with one shop and a simple online presence. We've talked about it and agreed that opening a second or subsequent shops wouldn't necessarily make us any happier.

It's all about balance. By running one shop between us we have the flexibility during the day to do things such as run errands, go to the gym or yoga, take a walk, or just disappear for a while if we want to.

In terms of a social life, I've had my times of going out a lot especially when single. But even then I loved nothing more than to be at home with the fire lit, knitting or reading. I knew I had to go out to meet someone though for they don't come knocking at your door, so I did what I had to (and actually met the perfect man for me, now my husband, in a bar).

It's not just about what I do for a job, or socialising though, it's everything in my life. I happily share one very ordinary car and enjoy creative and frugal pursuits at home. Expensive hobbies scare me.

Even though I enjoy the dream of living in or travelling to Paris or New York City, I love living in New Zealand and can't see myself living anywhere else. And for travel, I know it will come, I'm happy to forego it now, in this phase of my life where we are running a business.

If it sounds like I'm putting off happiness, I'm not. Every day I feel grateful and satisfied and thankful that I am where I am. I enjoy small luxuries frequently and make my own happiness. I collect simple pleasures such as going to bed early.

My Mum always said 'bored people are boring' when we complained of having nothing to do. I guess I took that to heart as now there aren't enough hours in the day for all the things I love to do – reading, writing, sewing, knitting, cooking, pottering, movie-watching – as well as living my everyday life in a thoughtful and stylish manner.

I no longer feel I have to apologise for not being a faster and more driven person. I am content to live my own life, at my own pace.

That's the greatest luxury of all I think: living a life custom-designed for me.

Living as our grandparents did

I've never really thought of myself as 'green', more 'old-fashioned'. But the more I research, the more I'm convinced they are almost the same thing. Our ancestors went about life in a thrifty and non-wasteful way. Meals were made from scratch, clothing was made and then mended, nothing was wasted and people read books for entertainment. This wasn't just a quaint notion, there really was no other alternative to all these things.

In my generation we went away from this in favour of conspicuous consumption. Thank goodness thrift is back in vogue again. Plus we have all this wonderful technology, so we really are lucky enough to have the benefit of both worlds.

Aside from the saving money aspect, I feel disrespectful if I waste food, or throw away something that could have been used by someone else. In fact I just can't do it. When we were moving house I drove my husband nuts, sifting through everything we were decluttering, figuring out where it could be donated to.

As much as I love those decluttering programmes on tv, it really upsets me to have the solution be a big skip outside, where everything is thrown in. If an item is in good, usable, clean, unbroken condition there is always someone who could use it that otherwise might not have the chance. I think it is our duty as a caring human being to try and find that person, via thrift shops, to charities that assist others or simply directly, by asking around.

Other ways I am like our grandparents?

I scrubbed our kitchen floor and entrance-way with hot water and sugar soap not long after we moved in (it was pretty filthy). Strongly-scented floor cleaners aren't for me. Normally I use hot water, white vinegar and a squirt of lemon dishwash. A few drops of essential oil are added if I'm in the mood. I also hang washing outside. And cook many of our meals from scratch.

Even when eating, the question could be asked 'would my Grandparents recognise this food?' when choosing what to eat. The world's population would be a much healthier place if we ate according to this.

Many of the ways in which our grandparents lived that are now trendy were originally done in the name of thrift or making do. I do these things to make the most of my resources, and also because I feel disrespectful to the Universe if I waste things.

I simply cannot throw something in the rubbish if it can be used by someone else (so I donate it) and I feel terribly guilty if I throw out food. If it's vegetation I throw out I feel bad that the Universe grew it for me and I wasted it. Even more guilt is felt if it's meat or eggs I throw out. An animal died (or laid) for me and I can't even be bothered to appreciate it?

As a result I throw out practically nothing. I honestly can't remember the last time I threw out food. If I don't eat something as leftovers for lunch the next day (like our creamy chicken and mushroom pasta from tonight, which I'll have with salad for lunch tomorrow), I will tuck it in the freezer to have another day. If it's something like a small piece of blue cheese or half a chopped onion, I will freeze to include in a casserole or soup.

Another aspect of living like our grandparents did is mending something if it's broken. There is much satisfaction to be gained from utilising our grey matter and working out how we can fix a problem. My sister was telling me today how she hemmed a pair of jeans shorter, and in the process used the excess denim to almost invisibly patch a hole in the knee. Result: one 'new' pair of jeans which are currently receiving a lot of wear.

I understand not everyone sews, but really, in the olden days it was just something you did. If one is really interested in living a thrifty life, at least knowing how to sew on buttons, hand-stitch a hem or sew up a small hole is mandatory.

Reading instead of tv watching, going for a stroll after dinner, eating real food, being a good steward of our finances, appreciating nature, growing herbs or even vegetables, making things with our hands: these are all ways we can enjoy life by living as our grandparents did.

Kaizen

I was talking with my husband about making our new (twenty three year old) home better over time, both with cleaning effort and low-cost updates. He then told me about *kaizen*, which is Japanese for *small and gradual improvement* and that's how their successful companies work.

I actually got very excited by this as it's how I live my life, and there's a name for it. How often does that happen? I don't really go for high-cost, high-maintenance but enjoy finding the do-it-yourself low-cost, creative route.

Because we are focused on paying our home loan off in a much shorter time than the standard twenty five years, we have decided to wait and see what improvements we want to do that require serious capital input.

We also practice this with our shop. I see other retail stores that spend big dollars on a fancy fitout (and make me feel like we should do the same) but within a few years have closed down.

Everything we do in our business we ask 'how many pairs of shoes do we have to sell to pay for this, and is it worth it?' Of course we have to be professional, but there are many, many ways to waste money I have found.

And we want our shop to be around for a long time. Being fiscally responsible is one way to ensure that as much as possible.

I often think imagine if you had a camera set up that took time-lapse photos of your home. It would show from the date you moved in how much better it looked month on month and year on year.

I'm sure 'kaizen' isn't a better known term (or maybe you've already heard of it) because it's not as exciting as the 'big reveal' of a makeover programme where everything is changed in an instant and everything is brand-new.

Just like a diet, slow and steady brings gradual and permanent change. As others have wisely noted in the comments section, our tastes change over time too, so if you redecorate your home all at once (obviously having just won the lottery), mightn't you get sick of it soon?

As with personal style, I think it's better to grow into your home look.

On living a low-key life

I read a book called My Friend Michael by Frank Cascio a while back, about Michael Jackson. His life sounded so glamorous being filled with first class travel, the money to buy whatever he wanted, fabulous hotels where he booked out an entire floor, not to mention being an international celebrity.

But sadly we all know how Michael's story ended. As he grew bigger and bigger he began taking prescription medicines just to cope with the stress of it all. Part of me wonders why he didn't downsize his life and just enjoy what he had, but as it was all he had known from age five, that thought probably didn't occur to him.

Besides, you don't get to be an international pop superstar by being a relaxed person who takes things in their stride.

As a side note, it was a fabulous book and I was really impressed by Michael's goal-setting and visualisation that the author described so well. The book is a good motivational tool. I made heaps of notes!

I have a cousin who, having just turned thirty is an extremely successful businessman that lives literally all over the world. He has two homes (Miami and London) and probably spends more time in hotel rooms and airplanes than he does in those.

He commented to a family member a while back that he feels sorry for me to be 'stuck' in our shop every day and never going anywhere. I was quite astounded when I heard that as I have never felt this way and don't consider our shop to be any different from other jobs I have had where I was obliged to show up at the office each day. It's just what I do.

An international life sounds glamorous and fun in theory, and I am definitely guilty of daydreaming when I see the celebrity photos of all the stars striding out from the airport gates (I have to process what they are wearing – cool sunglasses, check, leggings or skinny jeans, check, great jacket and loopy scarf, check).

But I am a home-loving person at heart who relishes routine and early nights, nesting and home-cooked meals. If I even have too many late nights I am all out of sorts.

And to do all these things that I love you have to have a job or lifestyle that means you can live in the one city and be home at a reasonable hour. I love that I spend each day in a familiar place and come to the same home each night.

When I go away on a rare holiday I just cannot wait to get home. Heck, even when I am out for the day I cannot wait to get home!

So I guess it's lucky I am not an international jetsetter then isn't it? But in the meantime I will enjoy perfecting the superstar travel uniform, just in case.

Simplicity manifesto

My idea of a minimalist has always been a free spirit who travels the world with only six items of clothing and a fancy Apple laptop in their backpack. I don't know why, it's just the image that pops into my head.

This makes me feel like a fraud when I consider myself a minimalist, but then just who decided the definition of minimalism and does it involve a certain number of possessions? Even though I know no-one decided, I do like this description from The

Minimalists (and funny that they mention the same thing I did about the stereotypical minimalist). They say:

Minimalism is a tool that can assist you in finding freedom. Freedom from fear. Freedom from worry. Freedom from overwhelm. Freedom from guilt. Freedom from depression. Freedom from the trappings of the consumer culture we've built our lives around. Real freedom.

And who doesn't want more freedom I ask you?

So I've decided to create my own definition of minimalism to help guide me to my own personal happiness.

Dave Ramsey has a great quote that goes '*live like no-one else today so that you can live like no-one else tomorrow*'. I love this saying and it really makes me excited at the possibilities I have for my life. It also keeps my encouragement up for living the way I do and having my own minimalist mindset.

I love that we are paying off our home loan much earlier than the standard 20+ years because it means we have more choices in the kind of work we do and how many hours we work.

I love that I don't need much to make me happy. I'm a real home-lover and relish time spent in my abode surrounded by the things I love such as books, music and creative projects. But compared with our friends, we don't have nearly as many expensive possessions.

My minimalism manifesto could equally be called a Simplicity Manifesto because I have such a beautiful craving for simplicity and it is actually one of my core values.

In putting together my ~~Minimalism~~ Simplicity Manifesto I will involve statements big and small such as:

I am intentional with what I allow into my life, whether it is an item, an obligation or a person.

I enjoy doing the laundry because I love everything I've worn and washed, and there is ample room to put it away when it is clean, dry and folded.

I will find magic in everything I do, because I want to live a magical life.

This is an ongoing project which I am enjoying working on!

A life of luxury

The word *luxury* is such an enchanting word, and there are many different meanings you can attach to it. I love to daydream about living a luxurious life. Yes, having material luxury goods is part of that daydream, but whether I am willing to pay for them and take care of them is another matter altogether.

On the rare occasion that I purchase a lottery ticket (maybe once or twice a year), it is a fun game for my husband and myself to plan what we are going to do with our winnings. That alone is almost worth the price of the ticket. We decide what we are going to do with the shop, where we will travel to and where we will live. We talk about what our new daily routine might be.

It is at these times that I reinforce to myself that we live a life of luxury already. Yes, we have to go to work, but how I conduct myself when I'm there, and what we do at home I encourage myself to do in a way that I think I would should I win that luxurious lottery lifestyle

Fresh fruit and vegetables every day. In the morning for breakfast a bowl overflowing with any of these, fresh and sliced – pineapple, strawberries, pear, apple, apricots, orange – topped with a handful of mixed raw nuts.

For lunch a luscious salad of lettuce, both home-grown and store-bought, home-grown fresh herbs torn on top, and any or all of sliced carrots, capsicum, celery, cucumber, tomato, then finished with good protein such as a couple of hard-boiled eggs, shredded roast chicken or tuna at a pinch and always avocado. Creamy dressings are my treat - I love Paul Newman's Caesar dressing and ranch as well.

In the evening a home-cooked meal, perhaps a roast? With roast vegetables and steamed broccoli, cauliflower and asparagus dressed in extra-virgin olive oil.

And of course glass after glass of fresh, clear, life-giving water throughout the day.

Am I in a fancy health spa or a top-notch country hotel? No! This is what I eat every day at home. I have gradually increased my consumption of fresh fruit and vegetables over time so that now the majority of my diet consists of them.

I am slowly and permanently ironing out poor dietary habits and changing them to new, healthy ones. As an added bonus, being slender and feeling vibrant is on my luxury lifestyle list too.

Spa-like pampering. Soft smooth exfoliated legs and arms, polished brightly coloured toenails, blow-dried silky hair and lightly applied make-up. I don't have to visit a spa for all these things, I just need to allow plenty of time in the morning to get ready (because I like to move slowly). I also remind myself that all these pampering things don't take very long, they are virtually free, and the results are worth it (I need that reminder on lazy days sometimes).

Having a leisurely start to the day. To have plenty of time to get ready in the morning, I made the decision years ago that I would rise at 6am every day, whether it was a work day or a day at home. It's better for your body to get up at the same time every day. It doesn't have to be 6am, but that's what time I have to get up to get ready for work, so I do it on my weekends too.

If you get up at different times throughout the week you give yourself a form of jetlag. And I read recently that having greatly varying times of getting up and bedtime is worse for retaining weight, just another reason to set my alarm.

Always having an engrossing book to read, be it fiction or non-fiction. Having a rich inner life is the best way to live a luxurious life on little money, and a book is a great vehicle. I read from my current book or books every day, always with my breakfast, sometimes with my lunch, sometimes before dinner, and definitely in bed when I retire for the evening. I don't often buy a book straight away, instead I borrow from the library first and then buy new if I like it enough for my personal library at home. I also browse charity stores and can pick up great books from there. They aren't usually more than a dollar or two. Sometimes they are keepers and sometimes I read and re-donate.

Beautiful music as my personal soundtrack.
I have many playlists on my iPod that I play at home depending on my mood. There are Buddha Bar/Hotel Costes/Café del Mar ones for when I want to feel cool and connected to the world, Richard Clayderman and Carl Doy for when I want to feel hotel-ish when I am doing my housework, relaxing classical adagios to feel elegant and peaceful, jazz for dinner guests or lazy Sundays and many more. Music is a must in my luxury lifestyle.

Surrounding myself with beauty and order.
At home I prefer calming colours. Even something as pedestrian as a washing basket I chose white, so it would blend in in the laundry or when I am putting clothing away. I couldn't cope with a bright blue one for example. Picking up and putting away as I move around the house keeps things looking tidy and helps my serenity.

Always having space to put something away at home is luxurious to me, that is why I love decluttering so much. The satisfaction I gain from editing and organizing a space for maximum ease and future pleasure is immense!

A word from the author

Thank you so much for purchasing this book. I truly hope you enjoyed a glimpse into my philosophy of living simply and well.

I welcome feedback and would be grateful if you could leave an honest review at amazon.com.

With thanks!

Fiona

About the Author

Fiona Ferris is passionate about the topic of living well, in particular that a simple and beautiful life can be achieved without spending a lot of money.

Her books are currently published in five languages: English, Spanish, Russian, Lithuanian and Vietnamese.

Fiona lives in the beautiful and sunny wine region of Hawke's Bay, New Zealand, with her husband, Paul, their rescue cats Jessica and Nina and rescue dogs Daphne and Chloe.

You can find Fiona's other books at: *amazon.com/author/fionaferris*

Other books by Fiona Ferris

Thirty Chic Days: *Practical inspiration for a beautiful life*

Thirty More Chic Days: *Creating an inspired mindset for a magical life*

Thirty Chic Days Vol. 3: *Nurturing a happy relationship, staying youthful, being your best self, and having a ton of fun at the same time*

Thirty Slim Days: *Create your slender and healthy life in a fun and enjoyable way*

Financially Chic: *Live a luxurious life on a budget, learn to love managing money, and grow your wealth*

How to be Chic in the Winter: *Living slim, happy and stylish during the cold season*

How to be Chic in the Summer: *Living well, keeping your cool and dressing stylishly when it's warm outside*

A Chic and Simple Christmas: *Celebrate the holiday season with ease and grace*

The Original 30 Chic Days Blog Series: *Be inspired by the online series that started it all*

30 Chic Days at Home: *Self-care tips for when you have to stay at home, or any other time when life is challenging*

The Chic Author: *Create your dream career and lifestyle, writing and self-publishing non-fiction books*

The Chic Closet*: Inspired ideas to develop your personal style, fall in love with your wardrobe, and bring back the joy in dressing yourself*

The Peaceful Life*: Slowing down, choosing happiness, nurturing your feminine self, and finding sanctuary in your home*

Loving Your Epic Small Life*: Thriving in your own style, being happy at home, and the art of exquisite self-care*

The Glam Life*: Uplevel everything in a fun way using glamour as your filter to the world*

100 Ways *to Live a Luxurious Life on a Budget*

100 Ways *to Declutter Your Home*

100 Ways *to Live a European Inspired Life*

Printed in Great Britain
by Amazon